presented to

_____

For the two Daniels in my life who have taught me Geborgenheit:
my father and my oldest son.

Keeper of the Springs

INGRID TROBISCH

WITH MARLEE ALEX

MULTNOMAH PUBLISHERS · SISTERS, OREGON

Keeper of the Springs

published by Multnomah Gift Books,

a division of Multnomah Publishers, Inc.

© 1997 by Ingrid Trobisch, Photographs © 1997 David Bailey

International Standard Book Number: 1-57673-098-0

Printed in the United States of America

Unless otherwise indicated, Scripture quotations are from

the New International Version (NIV)

© 1973, 1978, 1984 by International Bible Society

used by permission of Zondervan Publishing House

Also quoted: The New King James Version (NKJV)

© 1979, 1980, 1982 by Thomas Nelson, Inc. Used by permission.

Printed in Hong Kong

For information:

Multnomah Publishers, Inc. Post Office Box 1720 Sisters, Oregon 97759

LIBRARY OF CONGRESS CATALOGING-IN-PUBLICATION DATA

Trobisch, Ingrid Hult.

Keeper of the springs / by Ingrid Trobish with Marlee Alex.

P.cm.

ISBN 1-57673-098-0 (alk. Paper)

1. Home economics. 2. Home—Religious aspects. 3. Family-Religious life.

4. Trobisch, Ingrid Hult. I. Alex, Marlee

TX147.T76 1997

97-15657 640—dc21

CIP

97 98 99 00 01 02 03 04 05 — 10 9 8 7 6 5 4 3 2 1

Haus Geborgenheit means Place of Shelter in German. It is the name I've given my nearly eighty-year-old farmhouse in Springfield, Missouri. And Shelter is the theme around which I've worked, written, and raised five children under the umbrella of a lifelong love with their father.

Families come in all shapes: un-coupled, married without children, single parent, blended, extended, and the traditional nuclear family. Regardless of the configuration, there will always be those individuals who are the home-keepers; tending the needs of the people they love and making home "Shelter", the place to which those people keep coming back.

On my property in Missouri, just a short walk beyond the back door, springs bubble up within the shelter of a large cave that is open, front and back. The cave forms an earthen bridge, under which the springs become a stream. In the early twentieth century, this place gave the area its address: Natural Bridge. It was used as refrigeration for a family of ten on the original homestead. I often go there to cool off on humid summer afternoons. The bridge shelters the legacy of a family growing up long before my time as well as my own memories and dreams. It nurtures my soul and my sense of place in this world.

Every person is a kind of bridge to the future, unalterably linked to the past through family. Each of us shelter springs of our own ancestral legacy, spiritual heritage, and personal value which eventually flow on to those who come after us.

Whatever one's age and from whatever kind of family, people thrive in Shelter or Geborgenheit.

What gives family a sense of Shelter? Why is it essential that someone become keeper of the springs of the heart? In these pages, look beyond hectic days and explore the possibilities of what this might mean for you. Learn how to preserve the treasure in your own backyard, maintain and protect the springs that flow throughout your life and under the bridges that love builds.

Note: throughout, the word Shelter has been capitalized, as are all nouns in the German language, to emphasize the sense of place inherent in the idea of Geborgenheit.

The supreme happiness of life is the conviction that we are loved.

VICTOR HUGO

Treasure Legacy

1

keeping faith and things

With joy you will draw water...

ISAIAH 12:3 (NKJV)

Everything in my three-story house has a story. It is bulging with memorabilia, framed photographs, and desks or tables holding an array of scrapbooks and journals. Nearly every room has at least one cozy corner where I drink tea with friends and neighbors, tell stories to my grandchildren, or write letters to people far away.

In spite of a busy schedule, I make time each week to organize my writing tasks, keep cobwebs off the books, and refill my vases with a few posies, from the garden in summer, the grocery store in winter. When my grandson visits, he always wants to come into my library-office downstairs to have his good night story. "Ingma," he said one time, "I love this room; there are so many things to see."

The things in my home are not collector's junk, the result of hoarding or cocooning; they are my lifeblood. "Just throw it away" people might say of certain objects, broken and mended. But because these things have been wounded in action, they are the more precious to me.

Brokenness is a symbol of some new value. A crack or chip or missing piece denotes that someone touched this, someone used it once upon a time. Each patch or dent says, there is a story here: another chapter in the context of our family history.

When floods hit Missouri a few years ago, close friends carried everything in box after box up to the top floor, away from the seeping water. I was thinking, Oh, what a mess!

But instead of asking, "Why do you have all this stuff in your house?" my friends said, "This is your gift."

Keeping is a gift of celebrating family. I often think of a woman as a steadfast rock in the middle of a stream flowing all around her. On the edge of life and death, whatever comes her way, not knowing what will come next, she finds a way to stabilize, to hold her place, to create an island of security as the tides and currents change. She keeps the faith and keeps the things that give her family a sense of continuity.

Life can only be understood backwards though it must be lived forwards.

SOREN KIERKEGAARD

I didn't always have a house with well-furnished rooms as a single woman I studied for two years in Paris, living in a small flat. Even there I surrounded myself with meaningful reminders of my pioneer roots in the United States: my Swedish grandmother's hand-sewn quilt, photographs of our home, my brothers and sisters and pets. Each new friend I made abroad brought sweet new memories. I placed picture cards in frames and decorated with fresh fruit and flowers from the marketplace.

After marriage, Walter and I started off in a thatched-roof hut close to a dusty African village. Our days were full, taking care of practical, spiritual, and sometimes medical needs of villagers. Our lives were geared around basic necessities. But we did have a nice picture to look at and a china cup and saucer for tea. It was the meaning we gave to things we did have that enriched our sense of place.

We made sure we had good books in different languages and some kind of music. We had a little wind-up phonograph with three records we'd rotate and a small pump organ. When we were able to get other instruments, Walter started a family orchestra. And always we had the stars. Each evening at dusk we would sit outside and watch them twinkle, fall, or move across the sky.

Many years later in Missouri, having raised our family after Walter died, I was given gifts of one vase after another. Friends knew my love for flowers, but I began to feel there was more meaning in the gifts. I looked deeper and realized I was chosen just to be a vessel, a keeper, and to hold the treasure of family and legacy brought down the years.

chosen to be a vessel

It is a human need to somehow create a record of our lives.
The more fragmented the life, the deeper the need. A journal
is a book about our daily journey. It will never be completed.
It will never be perfect. If you start your book with this in mind,
you are already on the right path. Have courage to write
about the little steps even when they seem incoherent and
haphazard. The rest will fall into place. ⸺ Writing forces
us to articulate our innermost feelings. We may have to
write to ourselves before we even realize what is inside us.
It can be like exploring a dark cave, rather scary at first,
if we have allowed busyness to determine the course of our life.
But consistent journaling lights up our way. Writing
is a means of stepping back and observing the true life-
giving springs of the soul. What makes you feel deeply?
What books, movies, people challenge and stimulate your
thinking? In which ways? How are you getting to know God
better? ⸺ Why not choose a theme for your journal?
Contemplate something God has created that is close to your
heart: Flowers? Birds? Hands? The stars? The desert? ⸺
Cut out pictures. Find quotes. Study your Bible concordance.
Look for symbols. Find your own words in response to every
picture and quote you include. Ask God to open your eyes in
a new way. Share your insights with friends. Write down their
responses. The journal will become a way of tying your
fragmented life together. A Shelter for your hopes, dreams,
faith, and the love with which you live your life.

KATRINE STEWART

living the seasons

Will I be submerged again...not only by distractions but by
too many opportunities? The multiplicity of the world will crowd in
on me again with its values weighed in quantity, not quality; in speed, not
stillness; in noise, not silence; in words, not in thoughts; in acquisitiveness,
not beauty. How shall I resist the onslaught? I will have to substitute
another sense of values. Island precepts, I might call them. Simplicity of
living to retain a true awareness of life. Balance of physical, intellectual,
and spiritual. Work without pressure. Space for significance and beauty.
Time for solitude and sharing. Closeness to nature to strengthen
understanding and faith. A few shells must be my island eyes.

ANNE MORROW LINDBERGH, "GIFT FROM THE SEA" (CONDENSED)

Outside my dining room window there is a tall linden tree. It is like the one Walter and I stopped to admire on our walks near Salzburg, Austria. The branches that bend down close and touch the earth remind me of him. I cherish the shade of this tree, comforted even in the grief of widowhood.

Beneath the same window are white marguerites or shasta daisies, planted in honor of my daughter, Katrine, who carried them in her wedding bouquet. And the sunflowers beyond the lawn I planted for one of my tall, straight, and durable sons, David. I have planted flowers to remind me of each of my children.

Flowers are like children. Someone needs to be their keeper. Someone needs to nourish and fertilize them in spring so they shoot up tall and healthy. Someone must be there to admire their blossoms in summer, to trim away what's gone brittle and dry in autumn.

Even in winter, all is not lost. There are opportunities for cultivating beauty. In winter our capacity to believe is challenged when life lies dormant. I use this season to dream of color and think of ways to plant rainbows in the lives of those I love. When one of my sons had a sad divorce, I wrote his ex-wife a letter. "I will still cherish the wonderful memories," I said. "The good things, we'll always have."

Perhaps this autumn I will plant bulbs for tulips to represent hope or to celebrate a beautiful granddaughter who happens to have Down's syndrome. Trees and flowers nurture my soul. I am pleased to be their keeper.

Inside my front parlor, furnished Victorian style and with a wing-back chair, I begin each and every day. I call the chair my Father Chair because it makes me feel safe like I did sitting on my father's lap. In that chair I read and dream, pray and think. I can't imagine starting a day anywhere else.

It has become important to me to create a sense of emotional safety in my home the way my father did. He had a way of making it happen; I could not sleep at night until he came and kissed me. I remember once, just once during the years before he died, not getting to say good night to him, not getting his blessing. Perhaps the greater the Shelter or family feeling children experience growing up, the more they'll miss it when it's not there, and as adults, the harder they'll work to create it around their own hearth. Those who have never had it may crave it more deeply yet.

I see many people hungry for this. Perhaps each one of us need more places in our lives with a wing-back chair where we can nestle on our Heavenly Father's lap. In the last decade particularly, I've observed women trying hard to manage everything by juggling responsibilities traditionally considered masculine. Many of them are not affirming their own need for intimacy and emotional safety. Many, attempting to be all things to all people, find it hard to become vulnerable like a child, accepting of soft strokes, warm words, and touch.

Each of us might find it a relief to lay down defenses and allow our mates and ourselves to be weak. It may mean listening more than we talk. Or if we are one of the rare breed of people who listen well, it may mean urging ourselves to talk more. If we are a natural giver, we allow ourselves to receive. If we are a taker, we concentrate on giving.

It's okay to open your heart, even if it must bleed a little. It's strength to admit when you're wrong and to apologize. It's strength to recognize how much you are able to love, beyond what you thought possible. On the other hand, it takes strength to recognize personal boundaries and pull them around you like a warm blanket. These are all ways to define Shelter.

By allowing vulnerable experiences in quiet and rest, you become a person who makes every context a safe place. Your life becomes Shelter—whether giving a good night kiss to a child or listening to the secret dreams of a spouse. It starts every day in your own wing-back chair.

the shape of family feeling

My parents worked many years to pay for the forty-acre farm where my brothers and sisters and I were born and raised. When Father died, my mother paid the last thousand dollars of the mortgage with his life insurance money, then gave our home away. It was to be used as a place of rest and recreation for Christian workers.

That old homeplace is adjacent to where I live now, in the house built by my grade school teacher's father-in-law. The surrounding estate of green fields has been divided now. But each plot of two to three acres is studded by huge ancient trees with sprawling branches.

When I purchased the home from Mrs. Crighton, my childhood teacher, she said, "I will sell you my house if you promise to do one thing every morning."

"What's that?" I asked.

"Stop whatever you're doing at ten o'clock," she told me. "Go sit on the front porch or backyard swing and just listen to the birds."

I have kept that promise. And I went a step further to keep a promise I made to myself. Included on my property was the original homesteader's cabin where the Crighton family lived before the rock house was built. "Tear it down," the neighbors told me when I bought the place. But something else told me to keep the cabin, to honor its legacy. I decided to invest my savings in preserving that little place even when the contractor said I was crazy. I asked him to save as much of the original wood as possible, keeping it in the style and colors of the late 1800s. Today the restored house stands in my backyard as a testament to this pioneer family who came from Scotland.

In John Steinbeck's *The Grapes of Wrath*, Ma asks a poignant question as her family leaves their Midwest farm to look for work: "Pa, how will our children know who they are if they don't know where they came from?"

Ma was concerned about losing family roots in the fragmentation of their lives. Her question has become my guiding principle as I've

where you come from

moved around the world. I've invested much effort in letting my children know where they come from and in helping them understand their legacy. We've always tried to show respect for the history of things and to honor peoples' stories.

Like a rock that doesn't budge in the middle of the stream that's flowing all around me, I reach out with one arm and touch my own heritage, pulling it to me. The home where I grew up now houses a flourishing ministry just as my parents envisioned.

With my other arm I touch what's happening in my children's and grandchildren's lives, the next generations. Some of them live in Europe where they grew up. They are musicians, doctors, theologians, diplomats, teachers, doing things I barely dreamed of.

I am one woman in the flow of history, using its momentum to define the substance of home. But every morning I stop; just long enough to listen to its song.

Cracking Nuts ❧ *A slow task. My thoughts speed ahead of my hands and long for faster results. I realize that in the realm of thought and spirit God has created me in His image. How easy it is to let my mind fly and race* *beyond the boundaries of time and of space. But the body lags behind. It is caught in the laboriousness of the task.* ❧ *To think that Christ voluntarily chose the confinement and limitations of a helpless body... ❧ I know beyond the shadow of a doubt that He understands how limited and slow I feel right now.* ❧ *Just cracking nuts.*

KATRINE STEWART

Remember that you can learn to delight in every obstacle God places in your path. Limitations force us to yield, to abandon ourselves to our creator, God. And when we do, his creativity flows!

JONI EARECKSON TADA

RootedRelationships
2

mother-hunger, mother-comfort

As a mother comforts her child, so will I comfort you.

ISAIAH 66:13

My mother was a down-to-earth sort of woman who taught her children cheerfulness, gratefulness, and hard work. But I grew up with a certain mother-hunger I could never explain. One summer evening when I was about twelve, I remember helping mother take down the clean dry sheets from a line strung between a hickory tree and two oaks in our backyard. All at once she stopped between sheets, put her arms around me, and gave me a squeeze. Her open expression of affection felt so good it took me by surprise. Later, when Mother and I were separated by continents, I was often warmed by the scent of fresh linens that brought the memory of her hug.

My mother surely never knew the depth of my mother-hunger. I can only wonder if I realized the depth of her affection. A process of inner healing has to take place for those who feel they've been kept at arm's distance. The expressions of love we long for from our mothers may never materialize in our lifetime.

In the shelter of a women's Bible study group I once shared a memory that blocked my flow of feeling toward my mother and for which I had secretly reproached her. Releasing that pain without meeting condemnation brought freedom and comfort.

My oldest daughter has spoken of her own pain about going to boarding school, saying, "I felt forsaken during those years away from home." And we, her parents, only wanted to give her the very best.

Mother-hunger is a private kind of hurt. Sometimes no one knows. But there is One who does, and He offers mother-comfort. The Bible tells a story of the prophet Elijah. Fleeing for his life, exhausted, he sat down under a broom tree and prayed for death. God didn't argue with him; He just did a motherly thing. He sent an angel, who touched Elijah and baked him a cake!

As a mother of five, even when missionary duties kept me from becoming everything I wanted to be, I've hoped, as my mother did, that my children know refuge in the safest place: under the shelter of the Lord's wings. Within His feathered nest.

Perhaps, in years to come, the scent of some favorite thing like fresh linens or cut roses in a vase may cause them to remember the warmth of their own mother's hug.

I have always been fascinated by hands. They are one of the first things I notice about a man. Upstairs, in my bedroom, I have a picture of a clay sculpture; a little girl curled up asleep in a large gnarled hand.

My father had beautiful, big, wonderful hands. He used them to bless his ten children. I remember the way he would hold objects from his childhood and missionary journeys and tell the stories behind them to my brothers and sisters. We still have a copy of The Koran my father received from a Moslem chief in Cameroon in exchange for a French Bible. I treasure Father's walking stick, too, a model of the one David Livingstone used along the route from Cape Town to Victoria Falls. My father used his along that same route.

And then, there were Father's books. He couldn't get his hands on enough of them. When other girls my age were hearing fairy stories, I was listening to him read about great adventurers, pioneering people who changed the world: Livingstone, Nightingale, and Goforth, a missionary in China. Even when our family car broke down and money was short, Father managed to bring home ten volumes of Junior Classics as a Christmas gift.

My father died in Africa when I was a teenager, just when I needed him most. He was buried in Dar-es-Salaam, Tanzania. I understand why he did what he had to do. He followed his vision and calling even when it was risky. Later, I put together the letters he had written with his big, wonderful hands and made copies for each of my brothers and sisters. They are his handwritten link to his children, grandchildren, and their children. They are what we keep of him.

I lost my father, but when I re-read his letters, I feel secure. I am the girl curled up in that gnarled hand in the picture. My father's hands stretch across my years of raising a family, ministering around the world with my husband, and now aging as a single woman; hopefully, with grace.

My father's faithfulness to God's calling was the foundation for my own calling. The strength and flexibility of his hands at work and play have inspired me as I go out to sow and harvest, then come back home to fold them in prayer or make a backyard picnic for a grandchild. Hands are the tools of one who is a keeper.

I have always been fascinated by hands.

the work of the father's hands

memories as treasure

When Walter and I were courting, much of it was through written correspondence. A vast ocean and two continents lay between us. When we became engaged, he was in Ludwigshafen, Germany, and I in Cameroon, French West Africa. I remember walking in the orange grove at the mission station the evening I received his letter asking me to marry him. I read his letter by moonlight, soft in the African night. The fragrance of orange blossoms wafted through the air.

But my heart rebelled. Is this the way to get engaged? I thought. At that time I began a suffering that was new to me: the pain of separation. At times it became a heavy ache in my heart. Still, even these moments were worth keeping and treasuring forever. I found joy even in the sorrow: the joy of becoming empty like an open hand. It was the joy of being no longer self-sufficient, but out of the whole heart, weak and longing. My soul became a vessel holding nothing, a vessel that can only wait until something be placed into it.

Walter wrote me from Germany, "Love is life with a pulsing heart. It is glow and storm and swing. It is life out of a strength that knows no end, being caught in the strong current of a river, carried to a goal the heart is longing for. Love is life straight toward God. Not looking too much to the right or left. Not mourning over that which is left behind. Like a ball whizzing through the air, it has a certain disregard for hindrances and unimportant affairs. Love leaves alone what is beyond our capabilities. But it is always dipping out completely the opportunities of the moment."

Today, I pick up three-years-worth of letters that crossed two continents between Walter and me before our wedding. Reading them recently for the first time in forty years, seventeen of which I have spent as a widow, I felt the same emotions as that day in the orange grove.

"I am falling in love with this man!" I told a friend. But again, my heart rebelled. The pain of separation became once more a heavy ache. Keeping sometimes hurts. If I could let go of the memories, if I had never held onto those letters, I could have avoided this ache.

But I embrace its bittersweet song just like before. For there is joy even in this sorrow, the joy of becoming empty like an open hand. Uncertainty and lonely longing are vessels into which God will place His providence and grace. These are new gifts to treasure.

Just days before my wedding to Walter in 1952 I boarded an Air France plane from Chad, West Africa, bound for Paris. The next morning I caught a train to Germany where I would see my fiancée for the first time in two years. Many worrisome thoughts ran through my head: This man speaks a different language than I. He grew up in a different culture. He fought on one side in World War II while my brothers fought on the other. Scars of that war were still evident when I looked out the train window.

Before arriving at my destination, I read a letter from Walter with the inscription, "Do not open until you are on the train." He wrote: "The person who will soon greet you is a man whose heart is overcome by the greatness of this moment. He is trembling as he thinks of the encounter with you. But in the trembling, there is a holy joy..."

Two weeks later this man and I were married. Four years later, we stood in dusty African soil and held our first child in our arms. Twenty years later, settled in Austria, we were raising five teenagers and ministering around the world.

Today, I savor the holy joy Walter spoke of. I have known trembling gladness and trembling sadness. My nest is now empty and so are my arms. But I hold them open to the future, for I know who holds it. I know the Master Keeper just as I knew Him more than forty years ago when I walked in the moonlight, soft in that African night.

I take God's letters, as I've done so many times, read them once more and allow them to become light on my path, for love is life with a pulsing heart...straight toward God.

MORE THAN KISSES, LETTERS MINGLE SOULS.

John Donne

There are many kinds of letters, including the obligatory and those you can't wait to sit down and write. In letters you explore the landscape of your soul and reveal it to a friend. Relating external events is fine and dandy, but is merely the ever-changing framework for another work of art being patiently completed within you. It takes courage and a quiet hour to find accurate words to describe your inner picture. ✒ Allow the outer events of your life to lead you inward. What has caused you joy, pain, or anger? A strong emotion you are willing to explore and articulate will lead you to an inner landscape. Emotions are good signposts along the journey. ✒ Sometimes the letter received from a friend wraps the soul in a warm blanket. Even the envelope is lovingly addressed by hand, the stamp carefully chosen and placed. It's easy to sift such letters from the daily avalanche of mail and patiently wait for the first uninterrupted moment to open such a treasure. Reading it is like opening a window with a striking view. What a luxury to think a thought to the end with pen and paper!

KATRINE STEWART

the balance of ritual

Walter and I were newly married and settled at our pioneer missionary station. We had a five-year term ahead of us, having left civilization as we knew it. Besides our ministry in Africa, we were supposed to build our own marriage by blending different cultures: German and American.

After ten days of this isolation in primitive conditions, Walter and I looked at each other and asked, "How can we survive?"

Somehow we did. And somewhere along the way, we realized we were not only surviving, but thriving. Walter and I eventually learned to blend the things offered by the union of our personalities and backgrounds. We learned to use the gifts each of us brought to the marriage and to establish comforting rituals in daily routine. The Shelter we built was broader and stronger than the thatched roof of our mud hut. Pooling our resources, we committed ourselves to home-keeping in the midst of manifold duties among the villagers.

I brought a love of art and color into our marriage. I had made a personal study of the way various cultures express themselves and I wanted to blend those in our first home. In France, where I lived as a language student, I noticed red was a favorite interior color and art is important on the walls of tiny apartment rooms, but socializing happens outside in sidewalk cafes. From my Swedish heritage I inherited a fondness for soft spring colors inside where social life centers around a candle-lit table.

When we went to Africa, I packed a pair of brass candlesticks and box of candles; we lit them even on warm African evenings. I also brought a French painting to hang on the wall of our mud hut, knowing a picture becomes a window to the world.

Walter brought into our marriage a great love for laughter, music, and literature. Weekday evenings he would read something aloud in French or German, like *Le Petit Prince*. We didn't always have to have something new. Friday night became fun night: we played games to keep sane. Walter always beat me at checkers. I usually beat him at any game depending on luck.

This blending and balancing of culture in daily life became ritual for us. Ritual is living in a kind of harmonious pattern. It is a spiritual discipline as well as a practical one. It is the first thing you teach a baby just out of the womb: to find the rhythm, to balance the body's needs (pleasure and pain) with emotional satisfaction. Emotional comforts consist of familiar sounds and tactile experiences like the softness of Mother's breast, as well as predictable experiences like the dawn after every dark night.

Ritual is an ancient tool to honor patterns in God's creation. It is a way to celebrate our lives, to create and to keep family feeling.

THE SKY IS THE DAILY
BREAD OF THE EYES
Ralph Waldo Emerson

Frequently we put our eyes on a starvation diet. Our sky has become the man-made ceiling of home and work. So step outside. Look up. Feast your eyes on the the always changing sky of the Creator of the universe. He will know how to nourish your soul. (You can practice this "heavenly discipline" daily when you take out the trash.)

KATRINE STEWART

into the light

In my home there are several paintings of women walking toward or into the light. In one, a North African woman is carrying a large bundle on her head. You see her from the back, tall and straight. I like the African way of carrying burdens. The straighter one stands, the more balanced the burden. With all the providing African women do, it's the way they carry the burden that conserves their energy for the important things. No matter how dark the day or heavy their suffering, they balance it with hope and keep on going.

Africans know how important light and Shelter, feeling safe, is for their children. I have seen it over and over when I lived among them. There is little neuroses among children in African villages because emotional Shelter is created by a balance of responsibility. From the moment a baby is born until age five or six his feet rarely touch the ground. Small children are shifted from lap to lap. They are carried, tolerated, and praised. They are not considered burdens. They are gathered into community around the fire.

And Africans know how to rest. When they gather around the fire circle, they bring their own pillows carved from wood. When someone gets sleepy, she just lies down, her pillow under her neck. I have a hand-carved wooden pillow I bought at an Ethiopian market. You can smell the smoke from a thousand fires in it. It reminds me of the words of Jesus, "Come to me, all you who are weary and burdened, and I will give you rest" (Matthew 11:28). This concept is well understood in the African village where comfort is often more spiritual than physical.

At a Family Life Mission (FLM) Conference in Nairobi many years ago, I heard an African bishop say, "You people from the West, stop dumping your garbage on us. We have something to teach you: respect for the family, respect for elders, respect for love."

And how to carry burdens, I think now. How to hold on. Go on. Walk on. Straight and tall, to face the dawn with courage. Then, at end of day, to share laps with children around the light of a village fire.

No mere willful activity whatever, whether in writing verses or collecting statistics, will produce poetry or science...all that a man has to say or do... is to tell the story of his love, to sing, and if he is fortunate and keeps alive, he will be forever in love. This alone is to be alive to the extremities.

HENRY DAVID THOREAU

3
Cherish the Present

from the inside out

Preach the gospel at all times. If necessary use words.

ST. FRANCIS OF ASSISI

I first met Walter's mother, Mutti, as we called her, at a cozy bed and breakfast near the Black Forest. She had managed to cross from East to West Germany during the communist border guards' lunch hour. Mutti spent several weeks with me before I was off to Africa as a missionary teacher. Each day she shared a little more about Walter's childhood. I got to know almost everything about his growing-up years, the happy days their family spent together before the clouds of World War II descended.

Two years after our first meeting, Mutti managed to pass through the Iron Curtain again, this time for my wedding with Walter in Mannheim, West Germany. At the reception she stood up, barely five feet tall, and announced: "I hereby renounce first place in the life of my son and give it to his wife, Ingrid." She gave me a sheltered position as helpmate for the man we both loved.

When Walter and I began our family, it was important to me to pass on the legacy of his German family to our children. Mutti had been a teacher and loved her profession. She used to say, "You don't teach subjects, you teach children." She had kept detailed journals and scrapbooks on Walter's life from the day

he was born. The observations she made and the mementoes in the scrapbooks fueled the imaginations of our children as they grew up, and now are available to our grandchildren when they come to visit.

After Walter's father died in Leipzig, Mutti was courageous enough to accept an invitation to come live with us in Africa. It was a difficult decision because, at age sixty-five, she knew she could never return to her home behind the Iron Curtain. She turned the key in the door of her apartment for the last time with only a small black suitcase in her hand. A few months after arriving in Africa she began to teach German in French to African students from thirty different tribes!

But most profound was the way Mutti influenced my life as a young mother. She made me aware of stages of development and learning in my little ones. When my third child was eighteen-months old, Mutti said, "Look! That child is like a budding flower; every day a new petal unfolds." From her sensitivity I learned to recognize one child's artistic nature, another's love for music, another's gift for hospitality. She helped me ask the right questions to bring out their different personalities.

Mutti taught me about making home a

castle, although ours was a mud hut at the time. In in her own war-torn Germany there had been no paint to fix up houses, so her people created coziness from the inside out. Mutti created a warm and soul-satisfying Shelter through the significance she attributed to little things.

A sense of Shelter is made when you put the welcome sign out in your face and life. Thoughtful, unexpected acts are welcome surprises. A gracious attitude toward offenses helps create family feeling. Everyone you meet carries invisible burdens. Sometimes people just get numb, but little things wake up love.

At the end of her life when Mutti became ill with heart disease, we cared for her in our small house in Austria. Our children participated in the process of letting her go. Beside her deathbed, they asked difficult questions: "Can she see us?" "Where is she now?" "Will we ever be with her again?"

A round-the-clock vigil of care was our first priority as a family. It was one more way to reverence who Mutti was, as well as our connection with the places, experiences, and lessons of hearth and home she taught us. Our five-year-old Ruth said to me, "When you get old, don't worry Mother; I'll take care of you like you took care of Mutti!" This is what legacy is all about.

BEAUTY SHOULD BE IMPORTANT AS AN
INSPIRATION TO DOING THE BEST WITH WHAT IS AT
HAND...EACH NEW FAMILY SHOULD PREPARE A HOME
WITH AS MUCH TO INSPIRE AS POSSIBLE.

Edith Schaeffer

How can our homes reflect a bit of the order and peace of
heaven? The shoes must be in their place, the dishes done, the
shirts ironed. But before we know it, we're spending so much time
keeping things in their place, we've lost track of our heart.
Plant a little ambience among mundane duties. At mealtimes,
enhance the environment and linger a while at the table: If you
have a fireplace, get a fire glowing before you eat: move a card
table in front of it occasionally. Or use more candles than usual
place them on side- tables, a couple at each
place setting, or on counter tops. ✑ Dim overhead
lighting and soften table lamps, draping a sheer-colored scarf over
the lamp shade (make sure it doesn't touch the bulb). ✑ Turn
on calming background music before you sit down. ✑ Decorate
the backs of chairs or sidetables with sprigs of greenery (ivy or
evergreen) and big bows made from complementary fabrics.
✑ Invest in a beautiful apron to use and wear when you serve
and sit down at dinner; apparel also creates mood. ✑ Keep
a flash camera nearby for dining room occasions; use it whenever
you have a guest or are celebrating a special event. ✑ Read from
enchanting books after dinner: an excerpt from a classic, a little
poetry, a line or two from a contemporary humor article,
something amusing from the newspaper.

MARLEE ALEX & KATRINE STEWART

the family circle

How different our lives are when we really know what is deeply important to us.

STEPHEN COVEY

Things that occur consistently within the family circle influence a child more than whatever happens outside. When family feeling is positive and strong, other influences can be neutralized.

In my childhood home, the art of conversation was taken seriously. Sometimes we would spend an hour after dinner talking around the table. I don't recall the little ones fussing. Mother would hold the baby and Daddy would hold the next and I suppose I'd hold the next. There was togetherness in it. Mealtime conversation bonded us and taught us to get along with all kinds of people once we were out on our own.

In the Walter Trobisch family, my husband would announce, "Children we're going to have devotions."

Our youngest, Ruth, would say, "Okay, but make it short!" And he did.

Walter and I sometimes underestimated our children, though, as I suppose many parents are prone to do. Our son David told me years after he was grown that I had underestimated his hunger to know God. He said I was giving him spiritual baby food as an eight-year-old when he was ready for more.

When we finally got television in Austria, our youngest was about six-years old. One night, there was a Shakespearean play on. We wanted to see it together but thought, Ruth won't be interested. We tried to get her involved in another activity. She soon piped up, "But Poppy, I want to see Spear-shake, too!" And she watched the whole thing. The circle of family feeling drew her in.

Sometimes I feel my own soul is either overburdened or undernourished. Life is not idyllic. It is not easy or always gratifying to be a keeper. There is a time—and I need it consistently—when the most important thing is to be quiet and create a Shelter for me. This is part of balance.

My children's friends from boarding school were talking about this safe place. They said that at school their beds and pillows were the only "place" that was their own, the only place they felt comfort. My daughter said she sometimes crept under the velvet blanket draping the grand piano in the music room. This was her place to be alone and think or cry or wonder. As lonely as their places were, they were still looking for that special feeling.

My sister, a missionary in Africa, told me the only "place" that belonged to her on furlough in Minnesota was her winter coat. "When I put it on I felt safe," she said.

My mother, an avid student, was given a beautiful old desk during the last year of her life. It was placed in a corner of the room she shared with another woman. "This desk is my hearth," she said at age ninety-two.

Each of us ought to learn the art of creating a safe place or hearth for our lives. This will change depending on where we live or how old we are, but it involves the idea of hostessing ourselves—treating ourselves as our own guest of honor. For me, this means taking a half-hour each day to drink tea in my nicest cup while listening to classical music or savoring words from a wonderful book.

Walking in nature has also become a regular part of caring for myself. I savor the sight and scent of trees and shrubs in the rolling hills where I live. I listen to quiet sounds. I look for signposts of God's creativity along Ozark roads.

The Danish philosopher, Soren Kierkegaard, said, "Every day I walk myself into my best thoughts. I know of no thought so burdensome that one cannot walk away from it."

When I'm burdened or merely busy with endless details of business and family, mini-retreats in places I love energize me. Enjoying a special nook or pathway alone draws me closer to God and replenishes my soul. Like a winter coat or a cozy corner to write, favorite places provide security and calm.

Welcome yourself into your home and life. Find one spot to call your own. Then build a fire on the hearth and keep it blazing.

a safe place

giving gifts to girls

In the days when the children were there to come back from school, they brought the world back with them. They brought tales of their adventures back with them to me whose only adventures most days had taken place inside my head. As surely as they brought back homework, they brought back home to that house, brought back more than anything else themselves to that house.

FREDERICK BUECHNER

Now that my three sons and two daughters are grown, people sometimes ask me, Which is more difficult to raise, boys or girls? I tell them, "Girls!" Because of the emotional roller coaster girls ride after the onset of puberty, everything tends to be a really big deal. Life can become very intense for a while.

Daughters who are first-born children are perhaps more difficult. But it's no fault of the girls. Sometimes mothers try so hard to do everything right the first time and in the process forget to have fun. My eldest daughter and first-born child, Katrine, was hard to reach emotionally as an adolescent. I believe it was because I didn't relax enough with her when she was very young. Perhaps, also, she didn't get quite enough of me when her baby brother came along. Once I told my sister I couldn't remember ever sitting on my mother's lap. She replied, "How could you? When I came along, I crowded you off."

Our second daughter, Ruth, was the last of five children. Her motto was "Me, too!" She exuded emotion. She could yell louder and climb higher than any of her brothers. In college she broke off a serious relationship with a young man because he didn't "have an ounce of feeling." Of the man she eventually married she says, "He can feel."

Birth order will have its influence, but regardless of that and other variables there are certain gifts I recommend mothers give every daughter. The greatest gift of all is respect for her daughter's personhood, from life in the womb onward. With so much new knowledge about prenatal psychology, we know earliest communication begins before birth. During each of my pregnancies I felt as if this child were called into being. I kept a separate journal each time. I looked for differences in personalities while carrying the baby inside me and thought differently each time about the budding life within. Sure enough, many of my impressions proved true.

Next to respecting your daughter as a person,

enjoying her is the most wonderful way to be a keeper of this relationship. There are boundaries to set and rules to police, but raising children is a process meant to be savored, not a goal to be attained. It's not about raising her to be someone, but simply to be who she is. Mothers who feel a sense of security about themselves: *I know who I am and where I came from* are best able to communicate: *I know who you are and I respect and enjoy you.*

The last great gift I will name is to watch over your daughter in prayer, then let her go. One daughter may be more difficult to release than another. You, as a mature woman, know that when your beautiful child steps out to make dreams come true, the stars in her eyes won't solve all the problems that arise. Still, you let go because, ultimately, you respect her. You love her enough to allow her to make her own mistakes, walk her own pathway, follow her own timetable.

Because you respect yourself, you allow your daughter the freedom to not live up to your expectations. This is the best gift of all.

EARTH'S CRAMMED WITH HEAVEN AND EVERY COMMON BUSH AFIRE WITH GOD.
Elizabeth Barrett Browning

Find a place where your thoughts can soar, your spirit can rest, your mind can slip into a realm of peace and abandon. Let yourself be surprised by the common things that God sets afire for you: morning sun on a piece of carpet, the silky fur of a kitten, the lingering scent of a spouse or child who has just left for the day. Give God thanks for every moment thus set apart. Ask Him to fill your waking (and sleeping) dreams with beauty, light, and vision. Walt Whitman says of such precious moments, "I loafe and invite my soul..."

KATRINE STEWART

Dance was not included in my pious American upbringing nor my international missionary training. But it was important to Walter who had learned ballroom dancing as a sixteen-year-old in Leipzig. Leading youth in folk dances while playing his accordion was one of his favorite things to do. As a pastor and counselor, he observed that religious people often seem least in touch with their bodies. Walter felt church-goers needed to cultivate a sense of harmony in this form of physical exercise that requires grace and precision.

It was not until I was forty years old, however, that I finally dared to learn. We were living near Salzburg, Austria, then, where ballroom dancing was part of our children's school curriculum. One time when Walter was going on a missionary trip for several weeks, I responded to an advertisement for a dancing course. A neighbor agreed to watch my children one night a week while, as a surprise for Walter, I attended a class in the city, and learned to waltz.

Dance set something free within me. It was like being allowed to skip and hop and run after being tied up for a long, long time. This physical discipline became a joy to my soul and brought a new dimension into our marriage.

Now, when my grown sons come home to visit, I say, "Before anything else, please, let's do a Vienna waltz."

MUSIC WASHES AWAY
FROM THE SOUL THE DUST
OF EVERYDAY LIFE.
Berthold Auerbach

Music is the language of brooks and waterfalls and springs gurgling on their way. Music is expressive of soul without the need for words. Every soul will find its own music. Music heals and mends and lifts heavenward. Music makes you want to dance and overcome the earthbound gravity of the moment. Music will draw you closer to the Creator of the universe. Find music that lifts your thoughts to heaven and play it during life's most dreary tasks. Perhaps you break into song while you empty the dishwasher, and your child asks, "What on earth is going on?" Let your heart sing for joy or for sorrow or for loneliness. Keep your soul dusted and your heart dancing through music.

KATRINE STEWART

God sets the solitary in families.

PSALM 68:6 (NKJV)

BrightCourage

explore your roots

A friend told me her grandmother's values were lost to her generation because her mother did not validate them. "I'm confused," she said. "I don't know where to find a role model."

Traditional roles, as important as they are, barely extend over a lifetime, let alone for generations. Changes for women involve many losses. Loss of community and support groups, spouse, children, jobs. They also include loss of ideals and illusions. There are times in our lives when we have to start from scratch.

I experienced terrible feelings of aloneness when I moved from my home of eighteen years and my comfortable circle of friends to a new home in a new country. No one in my new location had known my husband or children. My family had been a great part of my identity, but now I had to reach out to others as a single woman or be filled with self-pity.

How is it possible, I wondered, to be a keeper in our fast-changing society where all values seem to be questioned? Where roles are changing and evolving? Where the ground seems to shift regularly beneath our feet? Does starting from scratch mean throwing out the old? Forgetting history?

Dismantling our root system?

Simone de Beauvoir, a French author, was one woman who knew the wisest answers come from asking a better question. "It's the job of every woman to forget herself," she said, "but how can she do that if she doesn't know who she is?"

We are called to be human beings, not human doings. Normally, we get an education and learn, for example, to do medicine in order to be a doctor. But this is backwards. We must learn first to be in order to do. We must learn who we are. My friend who was looking for a role model started with herself and worked her way to the past, to her family legacy.

Listen to your personal gifts. Have you ever made a list of all the things you can do well? They are an important part of self-knowledge. Value your abilities whether they include organizing shelves and drawers, writing a legal brief, baking bread, making children feel loved, doing medical research, arranging flowers, or driving a school bus. Look for clues in the compliments of other people and in the things that make you feel relaxed and happy.

Then look over your shoulder. It helps to know something about the place you grew up and why your parents settled there. What experiences made them who they were? And what about their parents? Where did they come from? What were their cultural traditions? How did they celebrate holidays? What kinds of hobbies did they enjoy?

My great-grandmother came across the Atlantic on a small Swedish sailing vessel with four children in 1874. She and my great-grandfather had made a courageous decision to leave a settled, though limited existence to come to the vast prairies of Nebraska as homesteaders. He had to send her the boat fare twice from the new country because a swindler intercepted it the first time.

My grandmother was eight years old during this sea voyage. When I visited Sweden I found her birthplace, stood at the font where she was baptized, and located part of my identity there.

While my grandfather plowed virgin prairie soil in the Midwest, my husband's grandfather taught German to the famous boys' choir of Thomaskirche in Leipzig, where Bach is buried. Now all this is part of my children's and grandchildren's heritage, too.

Sometimes exploring our roots means we must make peace with our past and through forgiveness be set free from specific sins of parents or grandparents. It is not always an easy journey back. But as de Beauvoir implied, perhaps it is the only way to know who we are and then move on, to influence our world and the next generation.

There are times to go backwards and times to start all over again. Sometimes there is baggage to leave behind. Other times, there are threads to bring with us and weave into the tapestry of our future. I have known women who could not find a role model and so decided to be one. They prayed for discernment, sorted through options, and educated themselves in the school of life. They wove an identity with threads of past and present. They became be-ers and then do-ers in God's kingdom.

Set sail on your own voyage to a new land with fertile opportunities. Courage and patience will see you through until the seeds of your gifts take root, sprout above the surface, and bear fruit.

PICTURES SPEAK LOUDER THAN WORDS

Photographs can be a tangible way of reminding friends and family members they are loved and treasured. Pictures speak louder and more appealingly than words. By keeping and organizing photographs you affirm family belonging. ∼ There are many wonderful album and scrapbook ideas. But if you are tired of trying to keep up, don't. Create, instead, a photo filing box for each member of the family. Have reprints made to distribute into the various boxes. This system also makes it easy to "recycle" pictures for school and art projects or an interesting display of family history on the refrigerator. You will have a ready-made photo treasure box for each child leaving home. ∼ Organization keeps the pack-rat feeling to a minimum while helping to preserve your family history. Keep some tools like these handy: ∼ albums with plenty of room for add-in pages ∼ scrap books for newspaper/magazine clippings of favorite movies, significant current events and headlines, etc., to detail family history ∼ guest book for a record of friends and visitors ∼ prayer note-book with photos of those for whom you pray ∼ box of of cassette tapes with short interviews from family gatherings ∼ box videos shot at holidays, reunions, birthday ∼ box of family letters and eight-inch ribbons for tying into bundles; slip a photo of the letter-writer under the ribbon to identify ∼ baby book, school album, book of refrigerator art for each child ∼ a disposable camera in the car to record family activities.

KATRINE STEWART & MARLEE ALEX

the treasure of tears

Tears. You never know what may cause them.
But of this you can be sure: Whenever you find tears in your eyes,
especially unexpected tears, it is well to pay close attention.

FREDERICK BUECHNER

One of my secret wishes during the years I was the wife of Walter Trobisch was that one day I might see tears in his eyes. Although Walter had a happy childhood, he was taught that men do not display emotion. The war came (he was an eighteen-year-old infantryman in Hitler's army) and the battle of Stalingrad—too terrible to imagine, further stifling his ability to cry. Finally, Walter studied theology where again there was no place for feelings.

But I did receive my wish. When our third son, Stephen Walter, was born safely (I was flown out of a dangerous fighting zone during an African war), Walter wrote that he cried for joy upon hearing the news. Later, I saw my husband shed tears of grief for the choices our nearly-adult children were making.

One afternoon we talked about one of them and the pain with which we were wrestling. Walter pulled me close. I lay my head on his lap. Stroking my hair, he said, "Ingrid, just let the deep pain hurt."

Weeks later he died, and in the unexpected wrenching of his death, I drew comfort from the words he'd said that day: "Just let the deep pain hurt." Without being aware, my husband had prepared me for his departure from this earth.

Edith Schaeffer wrote, "Don't abort your afflictions." In other words, we do well to embrace the pain until its work is done. The human spirit in adversity can be a wondrous thing. Allow tears to flow. Scientists tell us they wash toxic chemicals from our bodies. Psychologists say they wash pain out of our hearts.

Tears are the price we pay for loving. Unless grief-work is done, a person is kept from being fully alive. "Blessed are those who mourn," the Bible says, "for they will be comforted," (Matthew 5:4). Mourning is never easy and lasts longer than most people expect. Often in the years following Walter's death, a memory, bittersweet and painful, would cross my mind. Unable to handle it myself, I would call a close friend who always listened patiently, let me cry, helped turn my eyes to Jesus.

Crying buckets of tears is a journey. It takes us from where we were before loss to where we'll be once we've adapted to the changes loss brings. No one can measure when those days are over. It requires patience with ourselves and with those who insinuate we should hurry up and get over it.

"A lady never hurries," says an African proverb. I believe patience is the continuous process of uncluttering what is around you and inside you. When loss is sudden and violent, it is like a bomb exploded in your soul. Picking through the rubble takes time. It is like looking for all the broken pieces of your heart. Tears wash away ash and cleanse your sight, making the important things easier to see. Tears wash away the dust of the trivial, the toxic, the temporary.

What remains is treasure. I saw it glisten more than once in Walter's eyes.

SOUL PROJECTS BRING A SMILE TO YOUR FACE, LIGHT TO YOUR EYES, NEW ENERGY TO YOUR HEART, JOY TO ALL AROUND YOU. SOUL PROJECTS ARE LIKE HEALING OINTMENT ON THE SORE PLACES OF YOUR LIFE.

Beethoven went for walks in the countryside. Golda Meir polished her silver   teapot. Josephine,   Napoleon's wife, tended   to her roses. Claude Monet gardened. Katharine Hepburn wrote her journal in bed with breakfast. Winston Churchill liked to paint. Einstein took long baths. Mendelsohn listened to the music of Bach. Mother Theresa listens to the silence of her soul.

KATRINE STEWART

always new beginnings

We live our lives in cycles. Our years may be divided into seven-year stages, each representing a new chapter of life: ⇍infancy to school age ⇍pre-adolescence ⇍adolescence ⇍young adulthood when most begin to put down roots ⇍the 30's when we send out new shoots ⇍the halfway mark for life expectancy; we gain a new stability ⇍the golden years when memories weigh heavier than dreams.

All life is a struggle for maturity through predictable events and un-predictable crises. We cannot afford to jump over any of its stages. They are all good, even the infamous midlife crisis, a time to evaluate and be renewed. Dr. Theo Bovet, a Swiss doctor, called meno-pause "femininity lost and then refound in a more wonderful way." In Africa a woman is considered a bearer of wisdom when she has completed menopause. It is the process by which a woman integrates all the stages of life.

Time does not stick around long, and there-fore I do not want to waste a single moment of it. I adhere to something I read from the pen of Eleanor Roosevelt: "If I have something to do, I just do it." Today, that's a multi-million-dollar slogan. It pays to contribute enthusiasm to whatever stage of life you are currently in. This is what makes the next stage fulfilling. You're practicing for your own future.

When discouragement strikes, remember: not one person on earth is immune to this human ailment. A favorite German proverb says, "That which doesn't kill me makes me stronger." There are times when God has to touch the tender spot in our soul. We may wince. But from the touching comes healing that makes us more beautiful and wonderful, ready for the next stage.

Martin Luther stated in his fourth thesis: "God's love is not a response to that which is worthy of being loved, but creates that which is worthy of being loved." God's creative love is a lifelong process. We are blessed that it accompanies us throughout each of life's phases and stages. His love never fails as we make transitions, endure growing pains, shed what no longer fits, and move into wisdom

A single burning candle can change the atmosphere in a room. Even by day I like to light a candle while sitting at my desk. It reminds me of the eternal values of light and beauty and perfection. It reminds me that there is so much more reason to keep on going than simply the next project on my desk. The candle is a symbol of eternity shining its way into my tiny corner of space and time. Place a candle on a mirror or in front of one to reflect and multiply its light. Along the center of your dining room table, candles create a glow on the faces of guests and family. A candle gives light only by consuming itself. In this way, it becomes a vivid symbol of the sacrificial love of Christ. By giving of Himself and His own substance, Christ brought light and hope into this world.

KATRINE STEWART

and maturity.

"Whatever things are lovely," wrote the Apostle Paul, "whatever things are of good report, if there is any virtue and if there is anything praiseworthy—think on these things... I know how to be abased and I know how to abound...I can do all things through Christ who strengthens me" (Phil. 4:8,12,13 NKJV).

God accepts us just as we are, but He loves us too much to leave us that way. He knows the only real mistakes we make are those from which we do not learn. He is standing by ready to offer a second innocence, a fresh start, a light on the path. Let us be a keeper of what is good as we carry on.

whole in brokenness

But Daniel purposed in his heart...

DANIEL 1:8 (NKJV)

The afternoon before Walter unexpectedly died, he and I walked together in the Alpine foothills close to our Austrian home. Only days before, we'd unpacked after three months of missionary travel which took us around the world. Quietly, on the trail leading through fields of wildflowers, Walter said to me, "I am homesick, Ingrid." He paused a moment then continued, "But I don't know for what. I am in the place I love most on this earth and you are with me."

The next morning after his usual run, Walter prepared a cup of tea for each of us and brought it to our bedroom, his usual custom. Setting the tray carefully on the table he said, "My body is trying to tell me something, but I don't understand it."

A moment later he drew his last breath.

There is a vacant spot in my heart still today, seventeen years later. It took great courage to accept my vulnerability as a woman. I had to learn to live in peace with myself despite the recurring ache of missing Walter. I took comfort in something a Jewish rabbi said: "There is nothing more whole than a broken heart."

Whatever does this mean? I wondered at first. Moment by moment and day by day, I found out. My discoveries are simple yet profound. They bring together humanity and divinity. They require a heart subtle as silk and a soul strong as diamonds. They unite hard work with perfect rest. They tangle together joy and pain. Wholeness out of brokenness, for me, meant rediscovery of simple pleasures.

Virginia Satir once said, "Every one of us has 13.5 square feet of skin—the largest organ of our bodies; and it's all full of holes aching to be touched." I often craved the warm clasp of Walter's hand in mine or the weight of his arm around me at night. After he was gone, I began to appreciate the feel of wild wind or gentle rain on my skin, the tickle of snowflakes on my face. I reached out eagerly to hug others and cherished each tight embrace with the innocence of a child.

I looked for beauty in unexpected places— like the smooth skin of a baby or the wrinkles of old age. I listened for it in requiems composed by the masters. I found it in the delicate fragrance of a breast-fed baby grandchild.

But wholeness out of brokenness is more. It is also letting go of places and people you cherish in order to move on. It is sifting through the important and separating the good from the essential. Wholeness out of brokenness means hard decisions and difficult tasks that only grief-work can help you finish.

When I left Austria and bought a home in Missouri, I packed the copper-studded trunk I used when leaving home on my twenty-third birthday. That trunk had known a place in an elegant Louis XV bedroom in the Latin Quarter of Paris. It survived the ravages of termites in the African bush. It had held my photo albums, journals, and wedding dress on its numerous voyages.

Now it carried to America the candlesticks that symbolized my home, the patchwork quilt my Swedish grandmother made, a vase or two from Europe, a few African carvings. I left much more behind, including the beautiful linden trees Walter and I loved, our neighbors, my children busy and working in Europe.

Moving on in life, wholeness comes in affirming everything and every place I have been as well as what lies ahead. This includes new qualities drawn to the surface in my character. A friend of mine told me, "Ingrid, you have said yes to your femininity. Now say yes to that gentle but strong Daniel in your heart," She didn't know that Daniel was the name of my father and my oldest son as well as the brave prophet of the Old Testament.

A Christian leader addressing singles at a retreat remarked, "We are all married. There's just the difference between the 'one-person couples' and the 'two-person couples.'" As my broken heart healed, I learned to understand what he meant and depend on the part of me that quietly continued to do what she had to do. Like other widows, I often felt invisible and uncertain. The temptation is to think I do not matter or I do not exist.

I have tried to nurture the daring Daniel in my heart despite the pain of isolation. These past years, I've planned and helped build a retreat center for family ministry on a quiet Ozark lake, hosted numerous guests in my home, traveled overseas and around this country. I've made new friends, written volumes, celebrated every milestone I passed. Each beginning moves me toward wholeness. I am keeping every golden moment, moving forward on a trail leading through fields of wildflowers closer to home. I have learned to bring Shelter with me and share it with others.

the mystery of connection